Graffiti

By Carmel Reilly

Illustrated by Diana Platt

Chapter 1 What a Mess!

One morning as Lily and Dad arrived at school they saw a group of people standing in the playground. The people were talking and looking at something on the side wall of the school office. Some of them looked angry and upset.

"I wonder what is happening?" said Dad.

Lily shrugged. She had only been at her new school a short time, so she wasn't sure what could be going on.

RULES
JUS
WAS HERE

As soon as Lily and Dad walked around the corner of the office they could see what everyone was looking at.

The wall was covered with graffiti.

Lily stared in amazement at the writing and splashes of black and red paint that were spread all over the huge white wall.

“Oh no,” she said. “What a mess.”

“This is terrible,” said Dad.

“Yes, it is,” answered the school principal who was standing nearby. “It seems to happen almost every weekend. We’ve had to clean this wall quite a few times now. I don’t know what we are going to do about it.”

Chapter 2
A Good Idea

At lunchtime it was sunny and warm. Lily didn't know any of the other children very well yet, so she sat alone outside on the grass to eat her lunch. She watched as her dad and some of the other parents cleaned the side of the office.

Lily saw a girl from her class called Meg. Meg waved and walked towards Lily.

"Can I sit with you?" she asked.

"Yes," said Lily, nodding.

"The graffiti looks terrible, doesn't it?" said Meg as she sat down. "I wish there was something that we could do about it."

Lily thought for a moment.

"I think there might be something we could do," she said, and she told Meg her idea.

TWISTER
54

That night at dinner Lily said, “Mum, Dad, could you help out at school soon?”

“What would you like us to do?” asked Mum.

“My friend Meg and I thought you could paint a big, colourful picture on the office wall.”

"You mean a mural?" asked Dad.

"Yes," said Lily. "We thought that might stop the graffiti."

Chapter 3
Working Together

The next morning at school Lily and Meg went to see the principal about painting the mural.

"I'm not sure," said the principal. "The paints would cost a lot. And the school council would have to allow it."

"Mum and Dad could come and talk to everyone. And they could also do a lot of the work," said Lily.

"My family could help too," said Meg.

"Lily, please ask your mum and dad to come and talk to me and we'll see what we can do," said the principal.

At the end of the week Lily's mum and dad came into her classroom to speak to the children.

"We've been talking to lots of people at school about painting a large mural on the office wall. The teachers and the school council have said that it is a good idea," said Mum. "What do you all think?"

The children were very excited. They all began to talk at once.

"And we want all of you to help," said Dad.

"Because we wouldn't be able to do a big job like this without you," said Mum.

The next Saturday the children and their parents arrived at school early to begin painting. With everyone helping, the mural was finished by the afternoon.

Lily and Meg walked to the other side of the playground so that they could look at the mural from a distance.

"It's so colourful," said Meg. "It looks wonderful."

"I hope the person who does the graffiti thinks so too," said Lily. "Then they won't paint on the wall anymore."

When Lily and her parents arrived at school the next Monday there were lots of people standing by the office wall.

“Oh no,” said Lily. “I hope there isn’t more graffiti.”

As they walked around the corner they saw the principal standing in front of the mural.

She smiled at Lily and her parents.

"This mural was a great idea, Lily. The wall looks beautiful. It's so full of colour. There is no room for graffiti here anymore."